NOW YOU CAN READ ABOUT...
CREATURES
of the
SEASHORE

TEXT BY KATE LONDESBOROUGH

ILLUSTRATED BY PHIL WEARE

BRIMAX BOOKS • NEWMARKET • ENGLAND

Some seashores are sandy. It is fun to make sandcastles. Do you know what made the footprints in the wet sand?

Where the tide reaches is called the tideline. You may find seaweed and empty shells. Be careful if you find jellyfish. Some can sting.

Here is a rocky shore. Cliffs rise up at the back. Look at all the birds on the cliffs. There are small animals in the rock pool.

Pebbles cover this shore. They are smooth. The small creature is a type of slug called a sea hare.

You will not see many creatures on a sandy shore. Most of them live under the sand. Can you see the lugworm? It digs a hole and leaves a pile of sand behind. This is called a worm cast. Shellfish also live under the sand. When the tide is in they suck in water.

The ghost crab comes out of its hole to eat seaweed and dead fish. Sandhoppers jump about. They look like shrimps. Look for the empty shells which are left when shellfish are eaten or die.

There are many kinds of seaweed on rocky shores. Animals hide under the seaweed. The hermit crab has no shell. The back part of its body is soft. Look for the hermit crab tucking itself into an empty shell.

This shellfish is called a piddock. It makes see-saw movements with its shell to wear away the rock.

Can you see the starfish in the
rock pool? It has strong arms.
It opens shells and eats the
shellfish. Barnacles cling to the
rock. When the tide comes in
they open their shells to feed.
Some fish live in rock pools.

In some hot countries the shore
is made of coral. Thick sea
grasses grow there. This coral
reef has many animals. Can you
see the small fish? It is cleaning
the big fish. The sea-snake eats
fish and frogs.

Sea anemones look like plants.
They are animals really. They
sting fish and eat them. Look
for the parrotfish. It scrapes
food from the rocks with its hard
jaws. Lobsters have ten legs. They
use eight legs for walking.

Many creatures live on mudflats where rivers join the sea. In some very hot areas mangrove trees grow in sea water. The creature on the root is a fish called a mudskipper. It comes out of the water and climbs trees. What other animals can you see?

Redshanks feed on shrimps and small worms. They push their long bills into the mud.

Herons wade in muddy water. The black heron has its wings spread round. It waits for fish to come near.

The fiddler crab lives on mudflats. Look for its big red claw. If the big claw breaks off, the smaller one gets bigger.

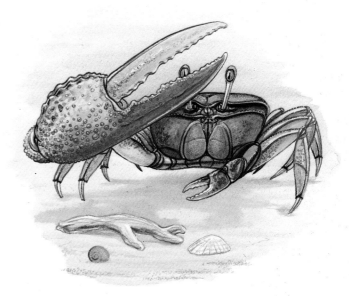

Some birds nest
on the seashore.
The ringed plover
makes a nest on
the beach and lays
its eggs in it.

Some pelicans
nest in trees.
Can you see the
chick feeding
from its mother's
mouth? The chick
has no feathers
when it is born.

Emperor penguins do not build
nests. The female lays the egg
and the male looks after it.
He rests the egg on his feet.
It keeps warm under feathers.
The male does not eat until
spring. Then the female returns
to feed the young penguin.

The polar bear eats fish and seals. Its thick fur keeps it warm in the cold sea.

Can you see the baby walrus? Its mother swims on her back. She holds her baby tight with her two front feet.

These baby sea lions love to play.
They jump out of the water and
splash down. Look at the sea lion
chasing a fish.

This elephant seal
has a large nose
like a trunk.
It eats fish and
crabs.

Turtles live in the sea. The female lays her eggs in the sand. She digs a big hole with her back flippers.

Look at the lizards. They lie on top of each other in the sun. They eat seaweed.

These otters live by the sea.
Look at them playing. They make
slides on a sandy bank. Baby
otters learn to swim on their own.

This otter is
opening a clam
shell. It lays on
its back and
bangs a stone
down on the shell.

Many sea birds nest on cliffs and catch fish from the sea. Look for the herring gulls. They have red spots on their beaks. Can you see the albatross flying? It flies for hours without beating its wings. The gannets are diving for fish.

Look at the puffins. They make burrows on the cliff top. Some birds nest on narrow ledges.

What kinds of seashore do these creatures live on?